UNCOVERING BIBLE TREASURES

31 GEMS AND JEWELS FROM THE BIBLE

UNCOVERING BIBLE TREASURES

DAVE STREHLER

Published in South Africa by Christian Art Publishers
P O Box 1599, Vereeniging, 1930

First edition 2002

Graphics by Michael Schoeman and Dave Strehler

Cover designed by Christian Art Publishers

Printed and bound by Creda Communications

ISBN 1-86852-987-8

02 03 04 05 06 07 08 09 10 11 – 10 9 8 7 6 5 4 3 2 1

Contents

Creation 1
Sin 5
God's enemy 6
Temptation 8
God makes a way 10
Jesus, the Lamb of God 12
Jesus is born on earth 14
Jesus died for our sin 16
He's alive 18
Jesus forgives 20
Go tell the world 22
Jesus goes back to Heaven 24
My new life decision 26
My helper 28
I'm free 30
Baptism 32
Growing in the faith 34
Talking to God 36
Walking in the light 38
The Bible 40
Ready for battle 42
God's family 44
Spreading the good news 46
Heaven and hell 48
The Lord's supper 50
Fruit 52
Serving together 54
A list of the Gifts of the Spirit 56
Jesus is coming for me 58
Our Father 60
Index 62

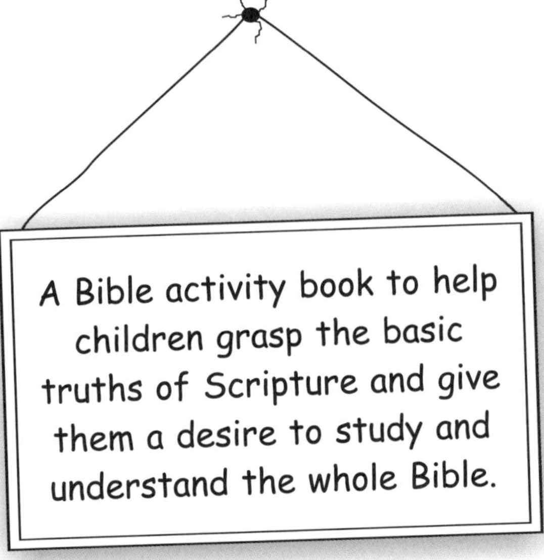

Hi there,

This book is written especially for you;
so write your name here:

____

If you'd like, you could use a pencil to do the activities, so that you can rub out the parts you may want to do again.

May God help you understand the important beliefs in this book, as you make new discoveries on your way from Genesis to Revelation.

'Treasure-hunt': Can you find a fish like this somewhere in this book?

CREATION

The word create means to make. Everything around us that God made, we call creation. When we want to make something, we need things to work with. Usually we need materials and tools.

Materials are things like clay, wood, paper, paint or glue that become part of what we're making.

Tools are things like hammers, saws, or scissors that are used to shape the material.

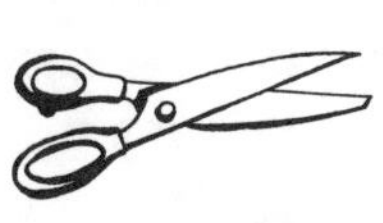

But ...

when **God** created everything, He started with nothing at all. All He did was **speak**, and things appeared just as He wanted them! On the next page are just some of the things He made.

Genesis 1, Genesis 2, Colossians 1:15-16

Can you spot the words in the block below. Circle them as you find them.

BEETLES
BIRDS
WORLD
ELEPHANTS
FISH
GRASS
INSECTS
LAND
LEAVES
LIGHT
LIONS
PEOPLE
PLANETS
SEA
STARS
TREES
WATER
WORMS

B	E	E	T	L	E	S	Z	F	C	W	Q	N	W	M
I	P	K	N	G	L	X	Q	I	H	O	B	P	A	T
R	M	I	N	S	E	C	T	S	W	R	Y	X	T	Z
D	S	F	G	H	P	W	Z	H	C	M	V	B	E	N
S	J	K	L	T	H	Y	P	M	L	S	T	A	R	S
J	K	L	P	L	A	N	E	T	S	Q	R	R	T	E
Y	H	G	F	B	N	V	O	Z	G	J	E	K	L	A
X	Z	R	K	L	T	H	P	G	W	F	E	N	M	D
L	E	A	V	E	S	Y	L	I	O	N	S	U	P	R
Z	O	S	X	C	V	B	E	W	R	S	G	L	B	C
T	M	S	N	H	J	C	B	V	L	I	G	H	T	X
U	X	K	L	Z	Y	L	A	N	D	R	Z	D	T	V

3

This is how it all began ...

Look up <u>Genesis 1</u> in your Bible to help you complete the words below.

On day	God created	Genesis
1	l _ gh _	1:3-5
2	sk _	1:6-8
3	s _ a, l _ nd, and plan _ s	1:9-13
4	s _ n, m _ _ n, and s _ _ r _	1:14-19
5	f _ sh and bi _ ds	1:20-23
6	_ ni _ als and m _ n	1:24-31
7	God r _ _ _ _ _	Genesis 2:2-3

Genesis 1, John 1:1-4

4

Wow! Imagine if you had been there when God put it all together. Well, you missed out on the first six days, but if you look around you, you'll still see the many things that God created.

Draw a picture of some things God created:

At first everything was just perfect, but then something happened. Read Genesis 3 to find out what went wrong.

Sin comes between God and us

Isaiah 59:2

When God created the first people - Adam and Eve – He let them decide whether they wanted to obey Him, or listen to the devil's lies instead.

God told Adam about the many things he could do and enjoy in the most beautiful place you can imagine. However, there was just one thing that God told him not to do. He was not to eat of the fruit of a special tree in the middle of the garden. But Adam and his wife Eve were both tempted by the devil to disobey God. They chose to believe the devil's lies and did what God had told them not to do. And so, by disobeying God, sin and death came into the world.

Since Adam, every person on earth has sinned by disobeying God - see Romans 3:23. Sin is the wrong, ugly things we do and think, even though we know they are wrong. We also sin when we **don't** do what God wants us to do.

God made a part of us to be like Him. We call this part our spirit because God is Spirit. But sadly, sin separates us (our spirit) from God - see Ephesians 4:18.

God's enemy – the devil

The devil was just an angel in heaven before he sinned by wanting to become as powerful as our mighty God. But God threw him down from heaven to the pit of hell like a bolt of lightning.

The devil now uses people to get back at God. Although the devil is God's enemy, he can never, ever challenge God's awesome power. All he can do is **tempt** you to sin, but he can never force you to do something you don't want to do!

Answer each question by putting a circle around the Y (yes) or the N (no).

Is the devil as strong as God?	Y	N
Can the devil force you to do something wrong?	Y	N
Is the devil more powerful than God's Spirit in you?	Y	N

Luke 10:18, Isaiah 14:12-15, 2 Peter 2:4

Here is a powerful verse from the book of James. To find out what it says, fill in the missing vowels (a,e,i,o,u).

S_u_bm_i_t y__rs_lv_s, th_n, t_ G_d.
R_s_st th_ d_v_l, _nd h_ w_ll fl__ fr_m y_u.

James 4:7

So...

With God's power in us, we need never listen to the devil or be afraid of him.

2 Timothy 2:26, 2 Thessalonians 3:3

8

Temptation - the devil's trap

Often we don't mean to do wrong, but somehow we mess up anyway. Temptation is the devil's way of trying to get us to sin against God.

Remember, temptation is not sin. It is only when we do what the devil tempts us to do that we sin against God.

What to do when you are tempted

- Run away from the temptation - 2 Timothy 2:22.
- Say aloud what the Bible says about that sin - Luke 4:1-13.
- Pray that you won't fall into temptation - Matthew 6:13.
- Don't stay around those who get you to do bad things - Psalm 1:1.
- Stay away from places where you could easily be tempted.

You can win every time!

2 Timothy 2:26, Hebrews 12:1, 1 Corinthians 10:13

Do the words below remind you of times when you've done wrong?

Join each word to its right meaning ...

Word	Meaning
quarreling	not telling the truth (or not living the truth)
cheating	taking something that doesn't belong to you
jealousy	fighting with words
hatred	secretly doing something against the rules
lying	praising ourselves for who we are or what we have
pride	being nasty because we want what someone else has got
stealing	having mean, ugly thoughts towards someone

These are just some of the things that make Jesus really sad. When we sin, we hurt others and make ourselves miserable as well.

2 Peter 2:9, James 1:12

God makes a way

God is so perfect and holy, that He cannot even look at our sin. This means that the sin in us keeps us away from God. Without God, our spirits are dead because only God can give life to the spirit in us.

But because God loves people and wants them to have life in Him, He let the people who lived before Jesus came to earth, kill an animal to pay for their sin.

God took the sin from the sinful person and put it on the animal. The animal was then offered on an altar and died in the place of that person.

But this way of taking away the sin of people was only for a while. It was a sign of what God was going to do. He was going to send His only Son, Jesus, to pay for the sin of the world - once and for all.

Isaiah 59:2, Leviticus 9:7, Hebrews 9:22

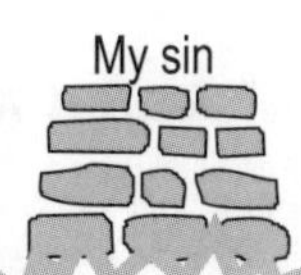

Copy the letters on the altar to the matching rocks below.

The animal became the ...

S _ _ _ _ _ _ _ _

READ ON ...

Jesus, the Lamb of God

God decided before He had even made the world, that at the right time, He would send His only Son Jesus to die in our place.

Jesus was the **only One** who could become a man and yet be sinless like God. That's why Jesus was the only One who could take our sin on Him and be punished as if **He** had sinned. In this way, our sin could be taken away at last, and God could look at us again, just as if we had never sinned.

And so, God sent His Son Jesus, from heaven to earth.

"For God so loved the world that he gave his one and only Son, that whoever believes in him shall not perish but have eternal life."
John 3:16

John 1:29, Revelation 13:8, 2 Corinthians 5:21

Find the only way that our sin can be washed away

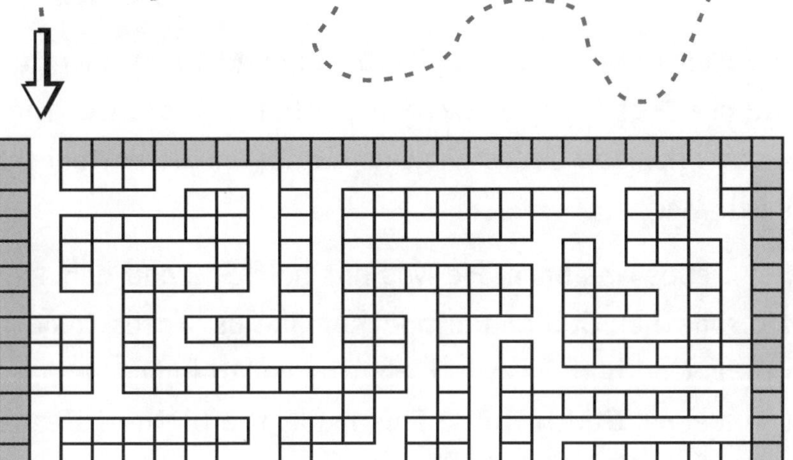

By the blood of Jesus

Psalm 51:7, Hebrews 7:25, Hebrews 9:24-26

Jesus is born on earth

For Jesus to become just like us, He had to be born just as we are. But there was one important difference: the Holy Spirit made Jesus grow as a baby inside His earthly mother Mary.

When Jesus was born, He was not half God and half man, but altogether God and altogether like us. Jesus came to earth as God had promised. He was called Emmanuel, which means: God with us. This made the birth of Jesus very special and very different.

Mary laid her baby in an animal feeding crib because there was no room for them in the busy town of Bethlehem. That night, God sent some angels to tell shepherds in a field nearby about the good news of His gift to all people. The shepherds went to see what the angels had told them and found Mary, Joseph (who had promised to marry her), and the baby Jesus wrapped in cloths - just as the angels had told them.

Isaiah 7:14, Micah 5:2-5, Matthew 1:18-24

Can you spot ten differences between the two pictures below? Circle them.

Some years later ...

Jesus became a young man. He chose twelve special friends to help Him spread the good news of God's love for people. But there were others who wanted to kill Jesus because they didn't believe in Him. They were jealous because many were starting to follow Him.

Luke 1:26 to 2:20, Isaiah 9:6

16

Jesus died in your place.

Jesus died for our sin

Bad men took Jesus and nailed Him to a wooden cross. As He hung on the cross He asked God to forgive them for what they were doing. The sin of the whole world was placed on Him. For that moment, God turned His face away from Jesus. The sky turned dark, and the curtain in the temple was torn from top to bottom. The sin that had kept us away from God was paid for, once and for all. Jesus took the blame for our sin.

*Greater love has no one than this, that he lay down his life for his friends. You are my friends ...**
Jesus

* (See John 15:13-14)

On that Friday afternoon, His friends buried Him in a tomb. A big round stone was rolled across the entrance. Jesus was dead.

But, that was not the end.

Psalm 22:12-18, Matthew 27, Mark 15

How does that make you feel? How about writing a letter to Jesus?

Dear Lord

....

....

....

....

....

....

....

....

....

....

Luke 23, John 19, 1 Peter 1:18-19

HE'S ALIVE!

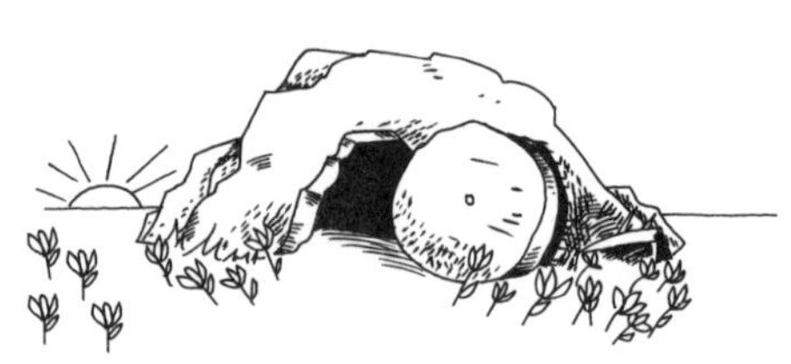

On the third day after Jesus had died, there was an earthquake and the stone across the opening of the tomb was rolled away by an angel. It was Sunday morning and Mary Magdalene was the first to discover that the tomb was empty. The two angels standing at the tomb told her that Jesus had come back to life. They said:

He is not here, He is ...

Draw a line from a-b-c-d-e-f, a-b, a- ... in each shaded block.

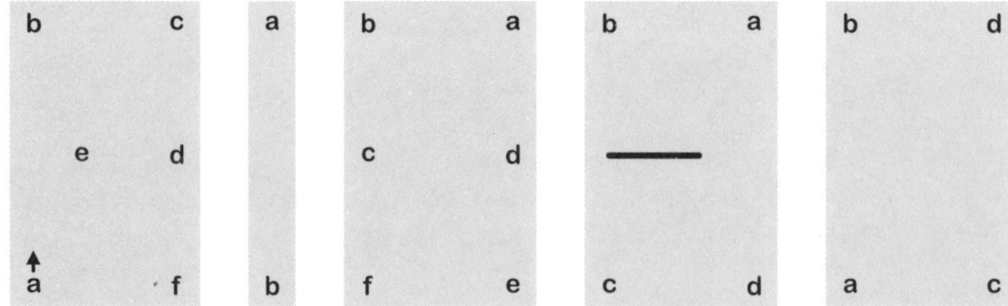

Matthew 28:1-10, Mark 16:1-8, Luke 24:1-12

Fri Sat Sun

~~1~~ ~~2~~ ~~3~~

Mary was a bit confused, but very glad. She ran back to tell the others that Jesus was alive. Jesus also showed Himself to two others who were walking back from Jerusalem to their village. When they realized it was Jesus, they also rushed back to tell the disciples that Jesus had risen.

He showed Himself to ...

To find out, unscramble the letters or look up the verses in your Bible.

_ _ _ _ .... arMy

_ _ _ travelers .... wot

_ _ _ _ _ _ _ _ _ .... sedcipsel

_ _ _ _ hundred others .... evif

Mark 16:9

1 Corinthians 15:6

Mark 16:12

Mark 16:14

John 20:1-18, Luke 24:13-45, Revelation 1:18

20

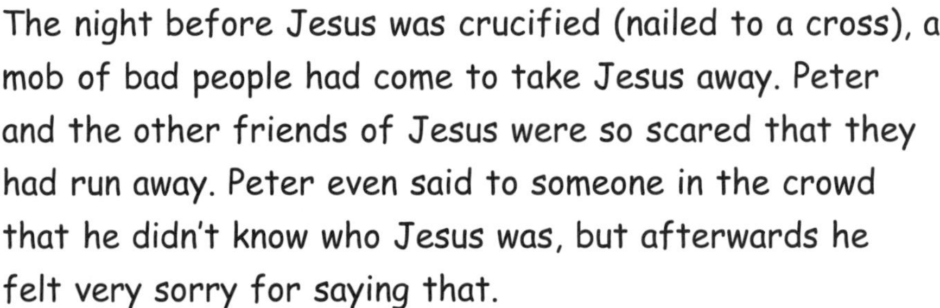

JESUS FORGIVES

But what had happened to the disciples of Jesus?

The night before Jesus was crucified (nailed to a cross), a mob of bad people had come to take Jesus away. Peter and the other friends of Jesus were so scared that they had run away. Peter even said to someone in the crowd that he didn't know who Jesus was, but afterwards he felt very sorry for saying that.

But now Jesus was alive again, and He wanted to show Himself to all His friends - especially Peter. He found Peter and spoke to him in a very loving way. Jesus still wanted to be Peter's closest friend and even asked Peter to do a special job for Him.

Jesus loves each of us in the same way and wants to forgive us for the times we've made Him sad. When you have done something wrong, you should always ask Jesus to forgive you and tell Him that you are sorry for what you did.

Isaiah 1:18, Matthew 26:69-75, John 21:15-19

What God sees when
your sins are forgiven.
(nothing but pure white)

Do you remember ...

- ☐ something bad you said?
- ☐ some wrong thing you did?
- ☐ being proud or jealous?
- ☐ not loving someone?

Sin makes us ugly on the inside

Circle the words that describe the way you feel when you've sinned.

bad
dirty
guilty
sad
scared

Ask Jesus to forgive you

(If you are not sure how to pray, turn to page 36.)

God promises that: * He will wash away your sins.
* He will never remember your sin again.

Psalm 103:12-14, Jeremiah 31:34

Go tell the world

After Jesus had risen from the dead He showed Himself to many people. Then one day, He and His disciples went to the top of a nearby mountain called the Mount of Olives. Jesus was going to leave His disciples and go back to His Father in Heaven. But first He wanted to tell the disciples something very important before He left them. This is what He said to them:

"Go into all the world and preach (tell) the good news to all creation (everyone)."
Mark 16:15

Since that time, this good news has spread all over the world and has reached you after many, many years. But Jesus did not only use special people to tell others about His love. He wants to use everyone who has become His follower. Just as you have heard or read the good news of His love, you too should pass it on to others - see page 46.

Can you figure out what we should do?

Use the secret code to complete the words below.

チ	=	A
ツ	=	B
ナ	=	E
ネ	=	H
ハ	=	J
フ	=	L

マ	=	O
メ	=	R
モ	=	S
ヤ	=	T
ユ	=	U

We should ...

ヤナフフ
T _ _ _

マヤネナメモ
_ _ _ _ _ _

チツマユヤ
_ _ _ _ _

ハナモユモ
_ _ _ _ _

Matthew 28:16-20, Isaiah 6:8

JESUS GOES BACK TO

When Jesus had finished talking to the disciples, He was lifted up into the sky and disappeared in the clouds.

While they were looking up, two men in white stood next to them and said, "Why do you stand here looking into the sky? This same Jesus, who has been taken from you into heaven, will come back in the same way you have seen Him go into heaven." Then the disciples went back to Jerusalem, joyfully praising God.

Jesus is in heaven right now, sitting on the right hand side of God the Father. He is always watching over you and listens to you when you pray to Him. As you pray, Jesus takes your place in front of God as if you were standing there yourself. Jesus really understands what it is like to grow up because He too was once a child like you when He came to earth. Read Romans 8:34.

Mark 16:19, Luke 24:51, Acts 1:9-11

Draw the outline of the letters covered by the clouds.

Jesus went back to ...

Color in the disciples
with bright colors

Hebrews 2:18 and 4:15, Hebrews 8:1-6

26

My 'NEW LIFE' decision

What must I do to have this new life in Jesus?

- **Believe** that you have sinned against God. (Romans 3:23)
- **Say** that you are sorry for your sins and that you want to stop doing wrong. (Acts 3:19)
- **Ask** Jesus to forgive you and make your heart clean. (Psalm 51:2, 7)
- **Trust** Jesus to free you from your past life of sin and give you a new life that goes on forever. (John 6:47)
- **Tell** Jesus that you want to follow Him, and let Him be Lord of your life - the number One in your life. (John 12:26)

A Prayer you can pray ...
Dear Lord, I believe that You came to earth to die for my sin. Only You can take away my sin because You are the Son of God. Please forgive me and wash away all my sin. Make me new and help me to follow You for the rest of my life. From this day on I want You to be Lord of my life. I love You Lord!

Amen

This is the most important decision of your life!

From now on ...

Pray often -
it's your 'hot-line' to Heaven - see page 36

Read the Bible -
it's your map along the way - see page 38

Join a church -
it's your new family - see page 44

Tell others -
it's your special assignment - see page 46

What to expect

Expect the Holy Spirit to fill you with Himself. God's Spirit comes to live in you - see page 28.

Expect to be set free from the **habit** of sinning. If you do slip up, ask Jesus to forgive you - see page 30.

Expect some problems and hard times. Life won't be easier, but you'll have Jesus to help you - see page 42.

Expect Jesus to come at any time just as He promised. He will fetch those who believe in Him - see page 58.

28

My Helper

Before Jesus left earth, He told His followers that He would not leave them all alone but send them a friend who would comfort and help them. So Jesus sent the **Holy Spirit** to help them, and all those who would believe in Him in the future. And now the Holy Spirit is not only in one place as Jesus was when He lived on earth, but lives in every believer.

Facts about the Holy Spirit:

- He comes alongside us when we are discouraged or sad and helps us through difficult times.
- He shows us what to do when we need to make important decisions.
- He helps us remember parts of the Bible we have learned. This is very important when we tell others about Jesus, or when we are tempted to do wrong (Luke 12:12).
- He helps us become more like Jesus by making us notice the things we are still doing wrong. He also helps us to want to be good.
- He helps us pray and makes God real to us.
- He gives us gifts with which we can serve others (see page 56).
- He is our proof that we belong to God (2 Corinthians 5:5).

1 Corinthians 6:19, Luke 11:13, Titus 3:5-6

Even though we cannot see Him, God as the Holy Spirit lives inside every person who has been born again and made new on the inside.

The words below remind us of the Holy Spirit.

Can you find the right place for them in the crossword?

ENCOURAGE
COMFORT
REMIND
POWER
GUIDE
WARN
REAL
HELP
GIFTS

Ephesians 1:13-14, Acts 2:3-4, Romans 8:9

30

Yipeeeee ...

I'm free!

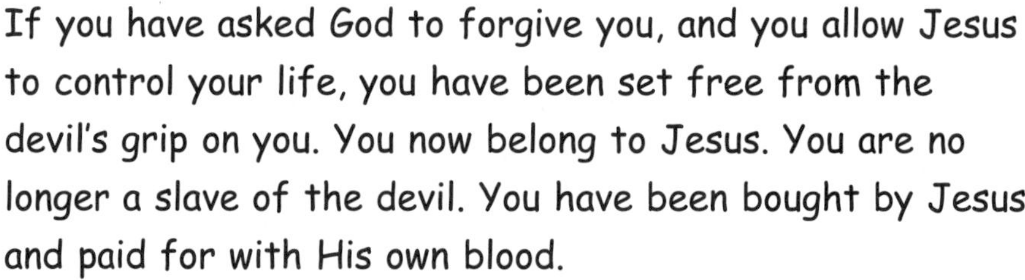

If you have asked God to forgive you, and you allow Jesus to control your life, you have been set free from the devil's grip on you. You now belong to Jesus. You are no longer a slave of the devil. You have been bought by Jesus and paid for with His own blood.

One of the devil's tricks is to remind you of the bad things you've done or tell you how bad you are. But ...

Remember!

The blood of Jesus has washed away all the sin you have done in the past and even the things you may still do wrong today, tomorrow, and for the rest of your life. You are free - a child of the King of kings!

Romans 6:6-7, Romans 8:2, Galatians 5:1

Even though the devil will still tempt you to go back to the old ways of sin, he has no power over you anymore. Jesus the King has set you free from the devil's grip and the **habit** of sinning.

The key verse has set someone free.
Who is it? ______________

John 8:36

If the Son sets you free, you will be free indeed.

Follow the chain ...

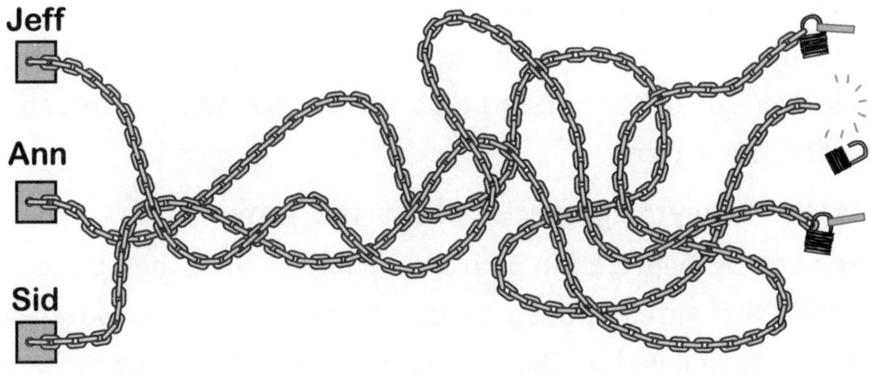

Hebrews 2:14-15, Romans 6:17-18

32

BAPTISM

What is baptism?

Baptism is a sign to show others that you are a follower of Jesus. It shows that your old life of sin has died and is buried with Jesus as you go under the water, and that you have risen to a new life in Jesus as you come up out of the water.

Who should be baptized?

A person who believes that Jesus is the Son of God, and has become a follower of Jesus.

How is a person baptized?

The person being baptized walks into the water. A church minister (or other person) dips the person being baptized under the water.

Is there anything special about the water?

You can be baptized in a river, a pool, or any other place where the water is deep enough to cover you. The water is not special water. Baptism is just a living picture of what has happened in your spirit.

Colossians 2:12, Romans 6:3-5, 1 Peter 3:21

Join the bubbles in the right order to complete the verse -
Colossians 2:12

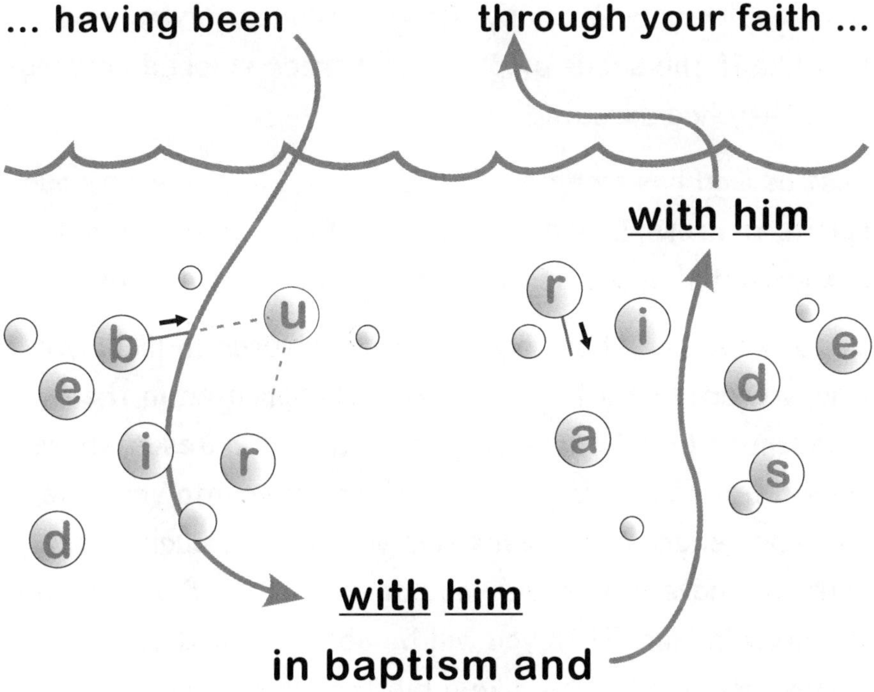

... having been **through your faith ...**

with him

b u r i e d

r a i s e d

with him

in baptism and

Matthew 28:19

Growing in the FAITH

'the FAITH' ... is what we as Christians believe.

Think what it would be like if you had stopped growing when you were a tiny baby. Imagine what a garden would look like if the seeds of plants and trees stopped growing once they had sprouted.

Just as God has made our bodies grow, He also wants our spirits to grow. This does not mean that our spirits get bigger, but that we become what God wants us to be.

If you have been born again by asking Jesus to make you new, you are like a tiny seed that has sprouted in the Kingdom of God. Your roots are grounded in Jesus where they can take up His goodness which flows into you. The love and goodness of Jesus fills your life through the faith you have in Him. As you put your trust in Jesus, you will grow in Him. Then you will be able to stand against temptation and trouble like a big tree in a storm.

Colossians 1:3-6,10, Ephesians 4:13-16

W_ _ _ _ _ _ _ _ _ _ _ _ _ _ _

_ _ _ _ _ **and he in us.**

Ways to grow ...

- ☐ Grow in the Word (get to know the Bible).
- ☐ Exercise your faith by trusting God in everything.
- ☐ Stay away from evil (bad things).
- ☐ Try to please the Lord in the things you do and say.
- ☐ Let your love for God and others overflow.
- ☐ Pray all the time.
- ☐ Listen to what the Holy Spirit is saying to you.

Romans 10:17, Psalm 139:2, 1 Thessalonians 5:22, 23

36

Talking to God

God loves to hear the prayers of His children. There always seems to be so much to talk to God about because nothing is too small to ask Him or tell Him about. Things that are important to you are important to God. He has time to listen to you for as long as you have time to talk. But even more wonderful is the fact that God is all-powerful and can do something about those things you chat to Him about. You can talk aloud to God or just think the thoughts you want God to know.

If you would like to pray to God but don't know what to say to Him, use the prayer that Jesus prayed when His friends asked Him to teach them to pray. Look up Matthew 6:9-13 in your Bible. This prayer will help you get started - then just carry on praying in your own words. The Holy Spirit will help you to pray.

John 14:13-14, Philippians 4:6, Romans 8:26

Jesus said we are His friends.

That means, praying is like talking to your best friend.

HERE ARE SOME THINGS YOU CAN PRAY ...

Tell God that He is wonderful
Tell Jesus that He is Lord of your life
Tell Jesus that you love Him

Thank Jesus that He died in your place
Thank Jesus that He has saved you
Thank God for the things He has given you

Pray for your parents
Pray for your friends
Pray for those who don't know Jesus

Ask Jesus to forgive you and help you not to sin
Ask Jesus to keep you safe
Ask Jesus for something personal

Jesus said that we are to pray to the Father using His name - (John 14:13-14). We can only go to the Father through Him.

John 15:14-15, John 14:6, John 16:23-24

38

Walking in the light

Have you ever tripped over something in the dark? Have you ever lost your way at night because you couldn't see which way to go?

In this dark world of sin, God has given us the Bible to be our light. The Bible shows us the right way to live and keeps us from getting lost in the darkness of sin. The more we use the Bible, the more clearly we can see the path that God wants us to take. The Bible was written by people who wrote down exactly what God wanted them to.

The Old Testament was written by prophets, leaders, kings and ordinary people who were used by God in a special way. All these writers lived before Jesus came to earth.

The New Testament books are mostly letters written to groups of people and churches after Jesus went back to heaven. God made sure that these special letters would be kept and added to the other writings to make up the complete Bible.

John 1:1-4, John 8:12, 2 Corinthians 4:3-6

It is always good to learn parts of the Bible off by heart. Here is a verse you could learn right now ...

Your word is a lamp to my feet and a light for my path.

Psalm 119 : 105

Book
Chapter
Verse

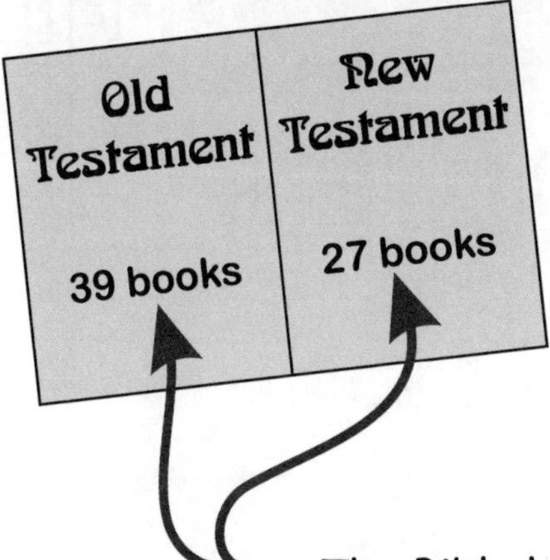

The Bible is divided into chapters and verses to help us find our way around in the 'Big Book'.

- The Bible has two main parts.
- The two parts are made up of many different books.
- The books have chapters.
- The chapters have many verses.

Luke 10:21, 1 John 1:7

40

The Bible

All these books in one big book - the Bible!

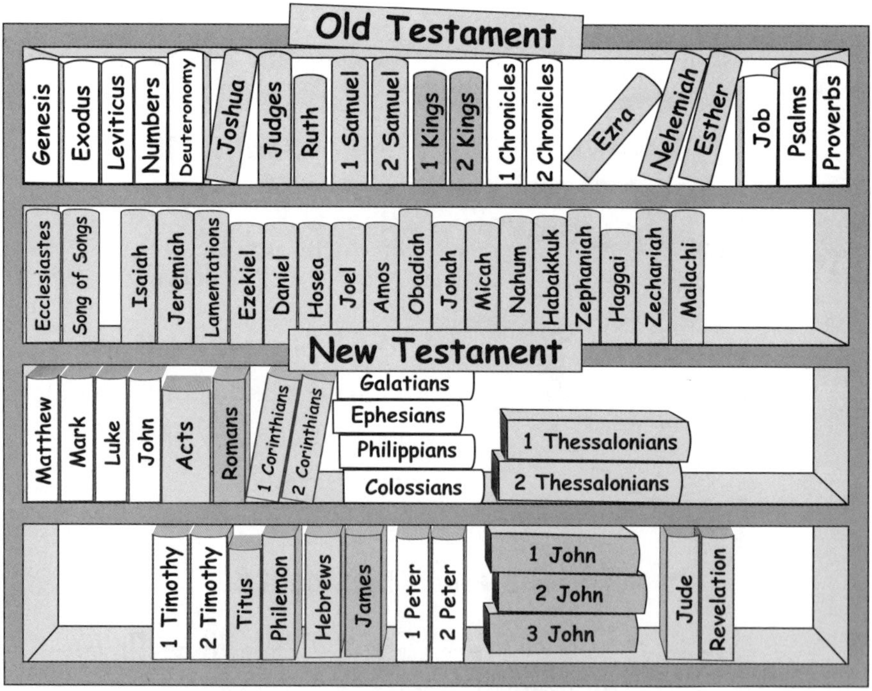

Old Testament

Genesis, Exodus, Leviticus, Numbers, Deuteronomy, Joshua, Judges, Ruth, 1 Samuel, 2 Samuel, 1 Kings, 2 Kings, 1 Chronicles, 2 Chronicles, Ezra, Nehemiah, Esther, Job, Psalms, Proverbs

Ecclesiastes, Song of Songs, Isaiah, Jeremiah, Lamentations, Ezekiel, Daniel, Hosea, Joel, Amos, Obadiah, Jonah, Micah, Nahum, Habakkuk, Zephaniah, Haggai, Zechariah, Malachi

New Testament

Matthew, Mark, Luke, John, Acts, Romans, 1 Corinthians, 2 Corinthians, Galatians, Ephesians, Philippians, Colossians, 1 Thessalonians, 2 Thessalonians

1 Timothy, 2 Timothy, Titus, Philemon, Hebrews, James, 1 Peter, 2 Peter, 1 John, 2 John, 3 John, Jude, Revelation

Important: If you cannot find a book of the Bible, look in the index near the front of your Bible. It will tell you the page number where the book starts.

Romans 15:4, 2 Timothy 3:15, Acts 17:11

BIBLE READING TIPS

1. Read a part of the Bible each day. You could start with Matthew, Mark, Luke, or John. Each of these books tells about Jesus.
2. Have a marker in the Bible to keep your place.
3. Write some notes about what you have read.
4. Ask God to help you understand the part you have read and ask Him to speak to you through the words.

The word 'Bible' appears 15 times in the square below. Circle them as you find them. The word may be written in any direction.

B	E	B	I	B	L	E	I
I	L	I	B	L	E	L	B
B	I	B	L	E	L	B	I
L	B	L	E	L	B	I	B
E	L	E	L	B	I	B	L
B	E	L	B	I	B	L	E
E	L	B	I	B	L	E	B

Luke 24:45, Psalm 119:11, 50, 160

Ready for battle

When you ask Jesus to be Lord of your life, it is like going over from the devil's side to Jesus' side. You cross over to the winning side to join many others who have also decided to serve King Jesus. As a soldier of the Lord, you get to use powerful weapons against the devil. Some weapons are used to defend you, while others are used to attack and destroy the work of the devil.

We don't use weapons like those used by armies to fight each other. Some spiritual weapons can't even be seen. God's weapons are used to fight evil, sin, and the tempting thoughts that the devil fires at us.

Even if you are young, you need not be afraid of the devil, because with Jesus in you, you are stronger than the devil. Remember, Jesus has already won the battle against the devil when He died on the cross to save us.

Romans 12:21, 2 Corinthians 10:4, 1 Timothy 6:12

Here is your armor:

See Ephesians 6:10-17

sh _ _ _ _
of Faith

_ _ _ _ d
of the Spirit

b _ l t
of Truth

h _ _ _ et
of Salvation

_ _ oes
of the Gospel

b _ _ _ _ _ plate
of Righteousness

2 Timothy 2:3, Psalm 28:7

44

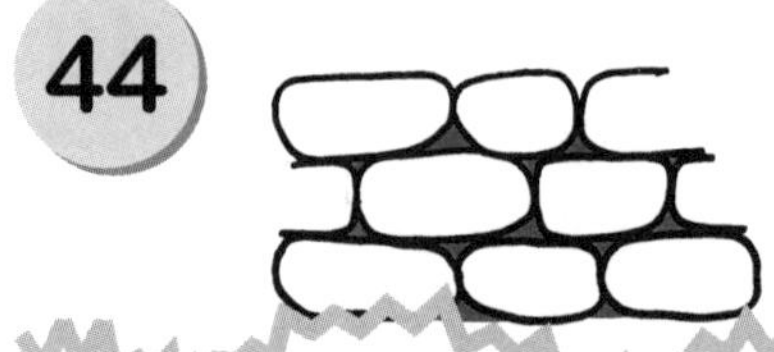

... you also, like living stones, are being built into a spiritual house ...
1 Peter 2:5

God's family

Jesus doesn't expect us to struggle on our own once we've decided to follow Him. He knows that we need others, and that they need us. He said that we should get together as often as we can, to help and encourage one another along the way. When we get together, we can learn more about the Bible from others, pray together, and worship God our Father in a special way.

All those who believe in Jesus are part of His body called the church. He is the head of the church and we are the body. This means that the church in not just an ordinary building, but is made up of everyone who loves the Lord.

Each one has an important part in God's living temple. God is shaping you to fit perfectly into a special part of His building like a living stone held in place by the love of those surrounding you. Together we are becoming a beautiful temple for God, with Jesus as the solid cornerstone.

Ephesians 1:22-23, Ephesians 2:19-22

We get together to:

- Worship and praise God (Colossians 3:16)
- Learn about the Bible (Colossians 1:28)
- Use our gifts to help others (1 Corinthians 12:4-7)
- Bring our offering to God (1 Corinthians 16:2)
- Work together to tell others about Jesus (1 Corinthians 3:8-9)
- Encourage one another (Hebrews 10:25)
- Pray for others (Matthew 18:19-20)
- 'Break bread' (have communion) (Acts 2:46)

◆ Draw a circle around the real church.

◆ The church is the _ _ _ _ of Christ (Jesus).

◆ Jesus is the _ _ _ _ of the church.

1 Corinthians 12:12-13, Colossians 1:18

Spreading the good news

When Jesus died on the cross, He died for the whole world - (every person). Yet many do not know that they can be saved and set free from the sin that rules their lives.

People need someone to tell them the good news that Jesus can set them free from sin and give them new hope. He gives living water to those who are thirsty for the right way, and rest for those who are tired of their life of sin. Jesus said that we should go out and tell everyone about Him.

How can God use me?

✓ Tell others how Jesus became your friend.

✓ Show them parts of the Bible that will help them find the way.

✓ Write a note or letter to someone who needs a true friend.

✓ Invite someone to your church group.

John 3:16, John 7:37, Matthew 11:28, Mark 5:19-20

Write the names of people you meet and places you go. Think about how God can use you to reach those around you with the good news!

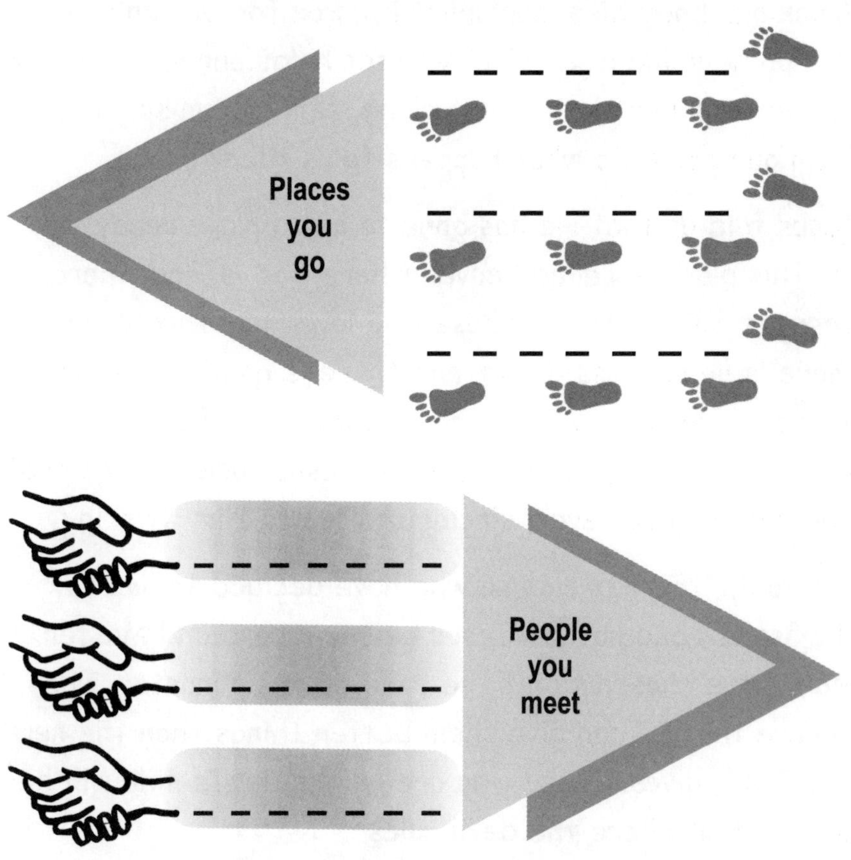

Romans 10:13-14, 2 Timothy 1:7-8, 2 Timothy 4:2

Heaven and hell

When our body dies, our spirit lives on forever and ever. Our body is like a jar of clay* that holds our spirit. When we die, it is like that jar breaking, setting our spirit free from our body. So what happens to us then?

Jesus told us that He has gone to get a place ready for us. This place is called heaven where God is, and where Jesus is waiting for all those who love Him. In heaven there is no sadness or sin, and there is no night because Jesus is our light. We will have new and perfect bodies that will feel no pain. We will see Jesus face to face and live with Him for ever, singing praises to Him with joy.

But sadly, there are some who have decided to live for themselves and not let Jesus be their Lord and Master. Many have chosen to let the devil be their master. They believe that he can give them better things than the new life Jesus gives. Those who are on the devil's side will be sent to hell where the devil rules.

***2 Corinthians 4:6-7, John 14:2-3, Philippians 3:21**

It's your choice

Hell is an ugly place where there is darkness, pain and sin, and from which there is no escape. But you can choose to make Jesus your Lord right now! - (see page 26).

Mark the boxes with a ✓ or a ✗

☑ ... will be in Heaven

☒ ... won't be in Heaven

- ☐ Jesus Rev. 5:13
- ☐ Tears Rev. 21:4
- ☐ Angels Rev. 5:11
- ☐ Sun Rev. 21:23
- ☐ Singing Rev. 15:3
- ☐ Night Rev. 22:5
- ☐ God Rev. 7:11
- ☐ Sin Rev. 21:27
- ☐ Joy Rev. 19:7

('Rev.' is short for the book 'Revelation' - the last book in your Bible.)

Luke 16:20-31, 1 Peter 1:3-4, Hebrews 12:22-23

The Lord's supper

(also called communion)

The night before Jesus died on the cross, He had a meal with His disciples. While they were eating, He took some bread and broke it to show them how His body would be broken on the cross. He passed the pieces around and told them to eat it. Then He took a cup of wine and passed it around for them to drink. He wanted them to understand that just as wine flows, blood would flow from His body to wash away all sin.

He told His disciples that from now on, they should have a meal like this whenever they got together so that they would always remember His death for the sin of every person.

This special way of remembering that Jesus died for us is only for those who love the Lord and understand the symbols of the bread and wine.

Matthew 26:26-29, Mark 14:22-25, Psalm 51:2

Draw a line from the pencil to the right symbol

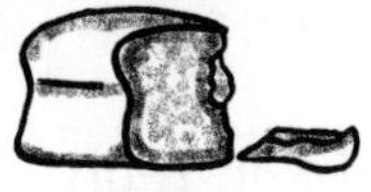

.... reminds us of His broken body

.... reminds us of His blood

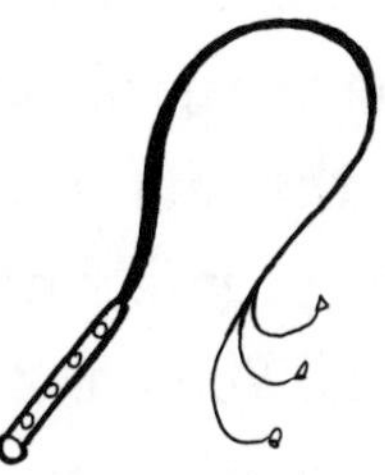

1 Corinthians 11:23-29

Fruit

Jesus said that He has chosen us to bear fruit. This is not the type you eat, but the type that shows the work of God's Spirit in our lives when we are rooted in Jesus. This fruit can grow all year round and never goes bad - it just lasts and lasts. You can even bear all the different kinds of fruit at one time. The fruit is the change that people see in your life when you become a child of God. The change starts in your heart which guides your thoughts and then grows into a fruitful action.

Just as there are some trees that don't bear much fruit while others are loaded with juicy, ripe fruit, we may need to check on the fruit in our own lives. How does your fruit show up in the different parts of your everyday life? Be honest with yourself and fill in the chart on the next page with a pencil. You can then rub out your score and try again in a few days' time.

John 15:16, John 15:2-8, Galatians 5:22-23

Rate your fruitfulness

Lots

Some

Little

These are the fruit of the Spirit

Love	☺
Joy	☺
Peace	☺
Patience	☺
Kindness	☺
Goodness	☺
Faithfulness	☺
Gentleness	☺
Self-control	☺

If you have not scored very well, don't feel bad, at least you deserve a high score for honesty. Pray about the fruit you are struggling with and ask the Holy Spirit who lives in you to help you. The fruit comes from inside you and grows as you let the Holy Spirit control and change you. If your heart is clean and your mind thinks of good things, others will soon see the fruit in you.

Philippians 1:9-11, Philippians 4:8

Serving together

The Holy Spirit has given you at least one special gift. When you were born again, He filled you with Himself and gave you a special way to serve others and honor God. Sometimes we only discover our gifts as we allow the Holy Spirit to use us.

Remember that we are servants of the King and servants of others too. Our gifts should never be used to please ourselves or make us think that we are better than others.

Spiritual gifts are not the same as our talents and abilities, although God can use these as well. We receive a spiritual gift when we give our lives to the Lord for Him to use as He wants.

The gifts we receive depend on how God wants to use us to help the church grow. Find a list of gifts on page 56 and 57.

Hebrews 2:4, 1 Corinthians 12:7-11, Ephesians 4:11-12

To complete the verse, write the word of each piece where it fits in the puzzle.

1 Peter 4:10a

received

he

use

serve

one

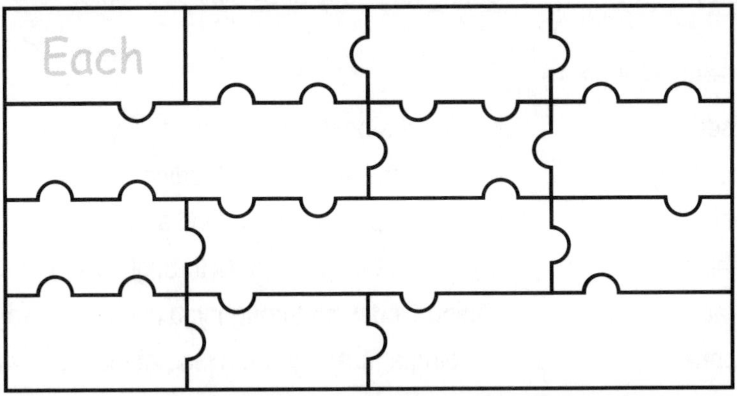

Each

whatever

Each

should

has

gift

others

to

A list of the

Gifts of the Spirit

Romans 12:6-8

⊙ Encouragement	Comforting and lifting up those who are down
⊙ Giving	Sharing freely and cheerfully with others
⊙ Leadership	Getting a group to do things together for the Lord
⊙ Mercy	Caring for needy and helpless people

1 Corinthians 12:8-10

⊙ Wisdom	Making the best decision in a tricky situation
⊙ Knowledge	Knowing the way God is leading
⊙ Faith	Having a special trust in God and His power
⊙ Healing	Bringing healing to others through God's power
⊙ Miracles	Letting God work through you in unusual ways
⊙ Prophecy	Bringing a message from God at the right time
⊙ Discernment	Knowing whether something is good or bad
⊙ Tongues	Praying in a special heavenly language
⊙ Interpretation	Explaining a message given in tongues

1 Peter 4:10, 1 Corinthians 12:14-27

shepherding

1 Corinthians 12:28

◉ Apostleship	Starting new Christian groups or ministries
◉ Teaching	Explaining the Word of God clearly
◉ Helping	Helping with the work of God in practical ways
◉ Administration	Planning and making sure that things run smoothly

Ephesians 4:11

◉ Evangelism	Telling the good news of Jesus to unbelievers
◉ Shepherding	Guiding and caring for 'younger Christians'

1 Peter 4:9-10

◉ Hospitality	Making others feel welcome and at home

Do you know what your gift is? Look at the list again and see which of the gifts gets you excited. Maybe you are already using your gift, but somehow you hadn't realized that it was really important. Write down the ways you would like to serve God with your gift.

____

____

____

____

Ask the Holy Spirit to help you recognize your gifts.

Are you ready?

Jesus is coming for me

Jesus promised us something very exciting! He said that He will come back to earth to fetch all those who believe in Him. He also said that He will come at a time when we won't be expecting Him. Jesus will come in the clouds in the same way His disciples saw Him go to heaven. When He comes, those who believe in Him will rise up to meet Him in the air with their new bodies and be with Him forever.

Those who don't believe in Him will be left behind and live through terrible times. It will be too late for them to change their minds - they will be judged and punished for their sin. Are you ready to meet Jesus if He came today? Let Him become your King today - see page 26.

Jesus said, "Here I am! I stand at the door and knock. If anyone hears my voice and opens the door, I will come in and eat with him, and he with me." Revelation 3:20

1 Thessalonians 4:13 to 5:3, 2 Peter 3:3-13

Split the words in the right place by copying the letters to the boxes below.

IAMGOINGTHERETOPREPAREAPL
ACEFORYOUANDIFIGOANDPREPA
REAPLACEFORYOUIWILLCOMEB
ACKANDTAKEYOUTOBEWITHME.

Jesus said:

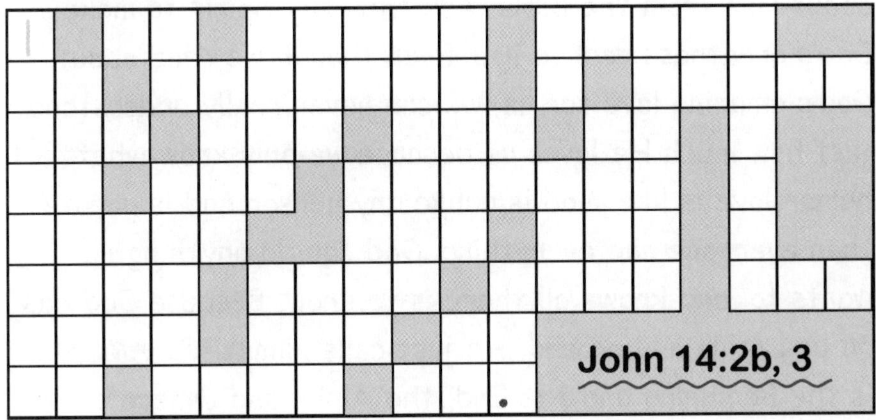

Matthew 24:36-41, Matthew 25, 1 Corinthians 15:51-52

Our Father

Have you ever wondered what God is like? Sometimes we let our thoughts and imaginations decide what God is like. We may hear people say things about God that get us thinking about Him in a certain way. You may think of God as someone who looks like a person, or even someone who is like your own father.

Although we cannot really know what God is like until we see Him one day, there are many things we can find out about Him from the Bible. Ask the Holy Spirit to make God's greatness real to you. Even though we read about God's amazing love for us, we can never really understand just how much He loves us because we only know what human love is like. God is unlike any person and is greater than everyone and everything. God can do anything He wants to, and knows all there is to know. Because God has no beginning and no end, He just calls Himself 'I AM'. He is the Beginning and the End; the Alpha and Omega*; the A and Z.

Exodus 3:14, Isaiah 45:22, *Revelation 1:8

Forever

Can you break the secret code? Write down the letter of the alphabet following the one used in the coded word. For example, A becomes B, B becomes C, C becomes D and so on - (Z becomes A). Each word tells us more about what God is like.

God is ...

LHFGSX	____________________	**Job 36:5**
LDQBHETK	____________________	**Daniel 9:9**
SQTSGETK	____________________	**John 3:33**
RSQNMF	____________________	**1 Corinthians 1:25**
VHRD	____________________	**1 Corinthians 1:25**
EZHSGETK	____________________	**2 Corinthians 1:18**
KNUD	____________________	**1 John 4:16**
KHFGS	____________________	**1 John 1:5**

A B C D E F G H I J K L M N O P Q R S T U V W X Y Z

Malachi 3:6, Psalm 145:8

Index

(For those who like using big words!)

Ascension 24, 25
Atonement 10, 11
Baptism 32, 33
Bible 38-41
Church 44, 45
Communion 50, 51
Creation 1-4
Crucifixion 16, 17
Devil 6, 7
Forgiveness 20, 21
Freedom in Christ 30, 31
Fruit of the Spirit 52, 53
Gifts of the Spirit 56, 57
God 60, 61
Great commission 22, 23
Heaven 48, 49
Hell 48, 49
Holy Spirit 28, 29
Incarnation 14, 15
Intercession (Jesus for us) 24
Jesus 12-25
Prayer 36, 37
Resurrection 18, 19
Salvation 26, 27
Sanctification 34, 35
Second coming 58, 59
Sin 5
Spiritual armor 42, 43
Substitution 12, 13
Temptation 8, 9
Witnessing 46, 47

Notes

Notes